CHURCH MUSIC SOCIETY PUBLICATION: 023A
Hon. General Editor: Richard Lyne

CONGREGATIONAL COPY

for the Choir and Congregation of St. Mary's Church, Nor

Saint Mary's Mass

Music by ANTHONY CÆSAR

Kyrie

Alternative version of Kyrie

Gloria

Glo-ry to God in the high-est, and peace to his peo-ple on earth. __ Lord God, hea-ven-ly King, al-migh-ty God __ and Fa - ther, we wor-ship you, we give __ you thanks, we praise __ you __ for your glo - ry. Lord __ Je - sus Christ, on - ly Son of the Fa - ther, Lord God, Lamb of God, you take a - way the sin __ of the world: have mer - cy on us: you are seat - ed at the right hand of the Fa - ther: re - ceive __ our prayer.

For you — a-lone are the Ho-ly One, you a-lone are the Lord,—

cresc. you a-lone are the Most High, Je-sus Christ, with the Ho-ly Spi-rit,

allargando in the glo-ry of God— the Fa-ther. A-men. A-men.

Gospel Responses

Glo-ry to Christ— our Sa-viour.

Praise— to Christ— our Lord.—

Sanctus – Benedictus

Andante solenne Ho-ly, Ho-ly, Ho-ly Lord, God— of pow'r and

più mosso might, heav'n— and earth are full— of your glo-ry. Ho-san-na in the

high-est. Bless-ed is he who comes— in the name— of the

Lord. Ho-san-na in the high-est, Ho-san-na in the high-est.

Acclamations

Agnus Dei

Acknowledgment

The *Gloria*, the *Sanctus*, the *Benedictus* and the *Agnus Dei* from *The Order for Holy Communion Rite A* from the Alternative Service Book 1980 are © International Consultation on English Texts and are reproduced with permission of the Central Board of Finance of the Church of England.

ISBN 0-19-395363-3

Origination by Jeanne Fisher, Ludlow, Shropshire
Printed by Halstan & Co. Ltd., Amersham, Bucks

Pack of 10 copies
Not available separately